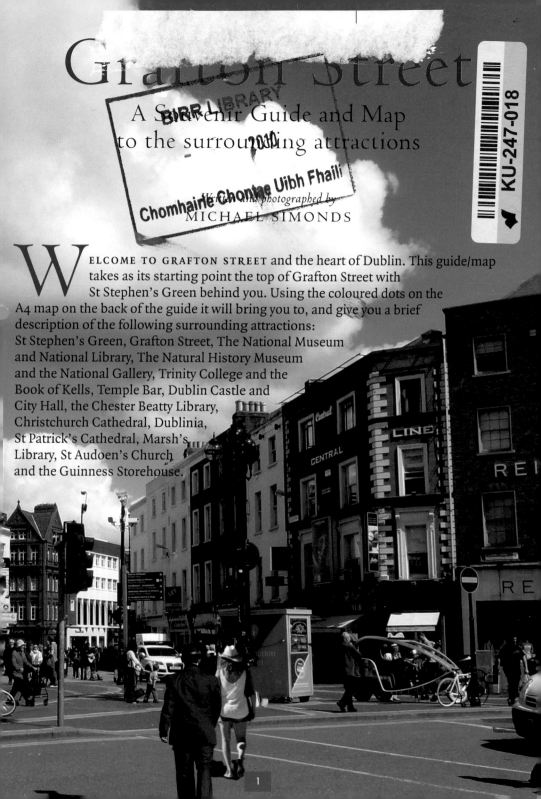

Grafton Street

A Souvenir Guide and Map
to the surrounding attractions

Written and photographed by
MICHAEL SIMONDS

WELCOME TO GRAFTON STREET and the heart of Dublin. This guide/map takes as its starting point the top of Grafton Street with St Stephen's Green behind you. Using the coloured dots on the A4 map on the back of the guide it will bring you to, and give you a brief description of the following surrounding attractions: St Stephen's Green, Grafton Street, The National Museum and National Library, The Natural History Museum and the National Gallery, Trinity College and the Book of Kells, Temple Bar, Dublin Castle and City Hall, the Chester Beatty Library, Christchurch Cathedral, Dublinia, St Patrick's Cathedral, Marsh's Library, St Audoen's Church and the Guinness Storehouse.

It is a subjective guide – each of the destinations provides its own detailed information and this guide is designed to get you to the attraction and give you its general background history. Our main aim is to give you a souvenir and memory of your trip to this part of Dublin. Pricing and opening times may change slightly and the timings given to get to each of the attractions are approximate. It is also worth remembering that on Sundays visiting times for St Patrick's Cathedral and Christchurch are affected by church services and that the National Museum is closed on Mondays, including Bank Holiday Mondays. You are on holiday and there is no rush, go and explore that side street, have a cup of coffee in a café or a glass of beer in one of the pubs. If you are on holiday in Ireland your time is your own.

St Stephen's Green

Starting at the top of Grafton Street you go across into St Stephen's Green and enter an oasis of calm and nature in the heart of the bustling city. Named after the medieval church of St Stephen that was located in the area, the land surrounding the church was originally commonage until claimed by the City Corporation in the 1660s. Building lots were laid out around the land and building was completed by the 1760s. Many of these original buildings have now been replaced by more modern buildings but some fine buildings still remain, one of the most outstanding being the impressive presence of the Shelbourne Hotel on the north side of the Green. At No. 9 St Stephen's Green you see the attractive facade of the Stephen's Green Club and to get a very good understanding of a typical Georgian house interior as well as seeing its exhibits it is worth visiting the Little Museum of Dublin at No.15, a short distance from the top of Grafton Street moving towards the Shelbourne Hotel.

The most dominant feature on the Green and at the very top of Grafton Street is the striking glass fronted Stephen's Green Shopping Centre. Looking like an enormous green house that incubates retail outlets it does have a definite presence even if it is not very sympathetic to the surrounding architecture. Opened in 1989 on the site of what was then a popular Dublin market, the Dandelion Green where U2 played some of their early gigs, it houses an interesting range of shops and cafés which add to the depth and variety of retailing in the Grafton Street area.

The fine arched entrance to the Green itself is known as the "Fusilier's Arch". Erected in 1907 it celebrates the soldiers of the Royal Dublin Fusiliers who fought and fell fighting with the British Army during the Second Boer War in South Africa 1899-02. Originally only available to the residents of the surrounding houses, the Green was opened to the public in 1880 despite issues from the surrounding residents over how the public would treat the Green and maintenance costs and outstanding

debts. Helping to deal with these issues and by providing funds to deal with the financial issues Sir Arthur Guinness was largely responsible for the Green opening to the public. Generations have enjoyed it since then and Sir Arthur Guinness, or Lord Ardilaun, is commemorated by a fine statue inside the railings near the Luas stop.

There are many other statues and monuments scattered throughout the park, James Joyce is here, Thomas Kettle, a memorial to W.B Yeats. The most striking are the Famine Memorial and the statue to the Irish revolutionary Wolfe Tone by the Merrion Square entrance opposite the Shelbourne hotel. Encompassed by its protective semi-circle of tall granite stone and designed by Edward Delaney in 1967, these two works well illustrate the different strands of Irish History and its complex history of occupation, tragedy and art.

To stroll around the Green on a sunny day, to enjoy the lakes and their wildlife, the sweeping lawns, the monuments and sculptures is a real

pleasure and a definite "Dublin" moment. It is also a fine tribute to the council's Park Service and the men and women of that department who maintain it. Hopefully it will continue to give pleasure for many centuries to come and with a nod to Lord Ardilaun you are ready to leave the peace of St Stephen's Green and embark on your exploration of Dublin.

of the 1850s it had assumed its position as the prime retail street of Dublin, a position it still commands today with its mix of major international and indigenous retailers.

Grafton Street

Named after Henry Fitzroy, the first Duke of Grafton (1663-90), he was the illegitimate son of Charles II of England. The title is still in existence and the present Duke today lives in Suffolk in England, a reminder of the complicated history of Ireland

with Britain and the British aristocrats who were involved in the building of Dublin in the Georgian period, many of whose names are reflected in the surrounding streets.

Grafton Street has always considered itself the premier retail street of Dublin, having an aristocratic street name gives it a head start. Originally laid out as a residential street in the early 1700s, by the middle

It is not possible to describe all the retailers on the street but some of the longer established ones stand out. Brown Thomas is one of the largest shops on the street and a Mecca for the serious shopper. Originally located on the opposite side of the street where Marks and Spencers now stands, it moved across to its present location in 1995 taking over the premises where Switzers once stood.

Brown Thomas was founded in 1848 by Hugh Brown who was joined by his partner James Thomas the following year. It was subsequently bought by Selfridges of London who ran it as a branch of their famous London business until selling it in 1933. It was then sold to a local Irish businessman and the company went public in the 1960s. Subsequently all the shares were bought by the famous Canadian businessman and philanthropist Galen Weston who had worked in Ireland as a young man in the 1960s. Interestingly his family also have a major shareholding in Selfridges.

Another famous name on the street is Weirs the jewellers. Founded in 1869 the family is still involved in running the business. Despite revolutions and Republics there was always some money in Ireland and in the shop's fine display windows this is where it most obviously manifested itself, and still does. And you cannot talk about Grafton Street without mentioning Bewley's Oriental Café, and its cosmopolitan clientele and history and its famous Harry Clarke stained glass windows. Opened by Victor Bewley in 1927 who had already established two other cafés in the vicinity, it was a rarity in the Dublin of those days in that it served a decent cup of coffee, the aroma of its coffee bean grinding machines giving that part of Grafton Street a distinctive smell. The group ran into financial difficulties in the 1980s and it was taken over by Campbell Catering who restored and rejuvenated the business. If you want your "Grafton Street" cup of coffee, this is where you go. The café is due to close in the first half of 2015 for renovations.

It is probably safe to say that all the

pubs on Grafton Street have literary and artistic connections. Dublin has always been famous for its writers, artists and dreamers. You have only to walk down Grafton Street and listen to some of the talented street performers to realise that the tradition is still thriving and it is a fair bet to say that few of those performers would turn down a drink if you offered it to them! But some pubs have stronger literary pretensions than others. On Duke Street, you will find Davy Byrne's and its famous connection with James Joyce's *Ulysses*. Opposite is the Bailey, both these pubs as well as McDaid's have strong connections with the literary circles of Dublin in the mid 20th century. Patrick Kavanagh, J.P Donleavy, Brendan Behan, Louis MacNeice, Michael Longley and many others, sung and unsung all drank here once. Most pubs have changed greatly over the years but to get an idea of the original character of the pubs of those days a visit to McDaid's on Harry

Street, just opposite Anne Street, is a worthwhile trip for an authentic Irish pub experience. Here also, just near the

pub, is a statue to the true Dublin Rocker, Phil Lynnot, forever standing guard over his beloved Grafton Street and the trendy Bruxelles Bar. Previously known as the Zodiac Bar this was a base for many of the Dublin groups of the 60s and 70s, amongst them Phil Lynnot and Thin Lizzy and it still claims many artists and celebrities as its clients today. Neary's on Chatham Street with its handsome facade is another popular pub. It is also worth remembering that Irish pubs are not all about alcohol and pride themselves on their food and coffee, there is no obligation to drink a pint of the black stuff or any alcohol. There are good pubs all over the area, they are there to be explored and enjoyed.

To find the more interesting local small businesses, go down one of the side streets and explore. Turning left down Johnson's Court, opposite the HMV store, and crossing Clarendon Street will bring you to Coppinger Row. Going down this to South William Street will bring you to Castle Market and its interesting variety of stalls and small businesses. Returning, you can come back through the Powerscourt Centre with its handsome entrance on South William Street. Originally the fine 18th

century Georgian Dublin home of Viscount Powerscourt, who built Powerscourt House in Enniskerry, it has been sensitively restored as a shopping centre and manages to mix Georgian elegance with modern retailing.

Grafton Street is home to many buskers and street artists who bring great life to the street, some are good and some not so good, but you never know, some of the performers play to a very high standard and you could be listening to a future international star! If you feel they are worth it give them an offering, they all add to the character of the street. There is also a considerable amount of begging on the street and the surrounding area. Mostly passive, some more direct, there are social services helping these unfortunate people so no one is going to starve. The best thing is to keep some small change about your person and if you want to help them give them something small, otherwise a smile and a shake of the head and you carry on. Another thing to remember is that there are few if any public restrooms in the area, if you want a wash and a brush, the National Museums and Galleries have very good facilities and you will also find washrooms on the top floor of the Stephen's Green Centre. Grafton Street is a place to stroll around, enjoy the crowds and the shops and recharge your batteries before heading out to explore Dublin.

1

To the National Museum and the National Library
(10 minutes walk from top of Grafton Street, admission free)

The National Museum. Open: Tues – Sat 10 a.m – 5 p.m, Sun 2 p.m. – 5 p.m., closed: Mondays (including Bank Holidays).
The National Library. Open: Mon – Wed 9.30 a.m. – 7.45 p.m., Thurs – Fri – 9.30 a.m. – 4.45 p.m.,
Open: Sat – 9.30 a.m – 12.45 p.m., open: Sundays (exhibitions only) 1 p.m.- 4.45 p.m.

Leaving St Stephen's Green behind you, you go down Grafton Street and take the first right down Anne Street. Cross Dawson Street and go down Molesworth Street opposite, ahead of you you see Leinster House, to the right is the National Museum, to the left the National Library.

Going down Anne Street, you see the imposing facade of St Anne's Church facing you after which Anne Street is named. Built in the 1720s by Joshua Dawson who laid out much of the surrounding streetscape and after whom Dawson Street is named, the Victorian facade was erected in 1868. Standing on Dawson Street and looking to your right, you can see the fine white building that Joshua Dawson built for himself. The building, known as the Mansion House, was purchased by the city in 1715 as the residence for the Lord Mayor which purpose it still fulfils today. In this house the first Dáil, or parliament, sat in 1919 when Sinn Féin won a majority vote after the election of 1918. Not recognized by the British Administration of the time it led to the War of Independence from Britain which led to the Irish Civil War which in turn led to the "Troubles" in Northern Ireland. So you are definitely in the centre of "Political Ireland".

Cross the street at the traffic lights and go down Molesworth Street. Dating from the early 18th Century the area was originally known as

"Molesworth Field". Lord Molesworth, whose father had come to Ireland with Cromwell, was involved in the early development of the area and it still possesses some fine Georgian buildings which give it a graceful air. Ahead of you, you see Leinster House, the seat of the Irish Parliament and the Irish Senate, or Upper House known as "The Dáil" . Designed by Richard Cassels, it was built in 1745 for the Earl of Kildare who became the Duke of Leinster. It was sold to the Royal Dublin Society in 1815 and they in turn sold it to the Irish Government in 1924.

Opened in 1890, the left-hand wing houses The National Library and the right-hand wing houses The National

Museum. The National Library holds much of the National Archive for Ireland and started life as the library for the Royal Dublin Society who then owned the building. As well as its collection of books, it holds census records, newspapers, historical photographs and much more besides making it a valuable resource for those people researching their family history as well as the general public. The Lawrence collection of photographs, held in the Photographic Archives in Temple Bar, gives a unique view of the whole country at the end of the 19th century. Much of this material can be accessed online on the National Gallery website which would probably be your first port of call if you wished to undertake research. The National Library also holds regular interesting exhibitions and has a café and shop on site. If you wish to access a book they have to be reserved and consulted in the handsome round reading room. The National Museum, which also started life as part of the Royal Dublin Society, has an extensive range of artefacts, all beautifully displayed, covering the history of Ireland from pre-historic times to early Christianity and the Vikings and the Medieval period. This is not really something you can write about, if you are in Dublin you need to see what is displayed and form your own impressions. The

displays are good and well described and somewhat like being in Egypt and seeing the magnificent antiquities there, you can get close to what was once part of the daily life of those peoples and their artefacts. The Museum holds some Egyptian and Roman remains but the majority of its collection relates to Ireland. The collection of Celtic gold on display is exquisite and the whole collection is a "must see" if you want to absorb some of the essence of early and later Ireland and what those people were capable of. Also on site are the museum shop and the museum café where you can pause to reflect on what you have just seen. Having absorbed some of the culture and history of the country you are ready to carry on with your exploration of Dublin. To visit the Natural History Museum and the National Gallery turn left at the exit and left again when you

reach St Stephen's Green and then follow the next set of instructions.

Courtesy National Museum of Ireland

2

To the Natural History Museum and the National Gallery

(Walking from the top of Grafton Street, 15 minutes, from The National Gallery/Library, 10 minutes)

Natural History Museum. Open: Tues – Sat 10.00 a.m. – 5.00 p.m., Sun 2.00 p.m – 5.00 p.m., closed Mondays and Bank Holidays, Admission Free.

National Gallery. Open: Mon – Sat 9.30 a.m – 5.30 p.m, Thurs 9.30 a.m – 8.30 p.m, Sun 11.00 a.m. – 5.30 p.m, Public Holidays 10.00 a.m – 5.30 p.m, Admission Free.

Standing at the top of Grafton Street facing St Stephen's Green, turn left, carry on along the length of the Green passing the Shelbourne Hotel until you join Merrion Row, take the first left down Merrion Street Upper and this brings you to The Natural History Museum and The National Gallery.

This is a great little walk that shows you Georgian Dublin at its best. Turning left at the top of Grafton Street you head in the direction of The Shelbourne Hotel and the galleries. Almost immediately on your left at no.15 you will see the entrance to the Little Museum of Dublin. This houses an interesting collection of artefacts and ephemera covering the social and political life of Dublin from 1900-2000. The house is well preserved and maintained and if you are interested in an original Georgian interior of a typical house on the Green, it makes the house doubly attractive. Open seven days a week there is a modest admission charge but it is a worthwhile experience. To get the full authentic experience of the interior of a Dublin Georgian house a visit to no.29 Lower Fitzwilliam Street (described below) is recommended.

Carrying on along the street you pass the impressive bulk of the recently restored Shelbourne Hotel. One of the premier hotels in Ireland, it was founded in 1824 by Martin Burke who acquired three houses and joined them together. These three houses

replaced an earlier house, Carey House, that was the residence of the Earl of Shelbourne after whom the hotel was named. He was another Cromwellian adventurer who at one stage was Physician-General to Cromwell's army but later settled in Dublin. It assumed its present appearance when it was bought by William Jury and Charles Cotton in 1865 who renovated it to the

highest standards of the day, which standard is maintained to the present time.

During the 1916 uprising, British soldiers in the upper rooms were able to snipe at insurgents who had taken up positions in the Green and forced them to move position. Today it is altogether a much more hospitable place.

Turning left down Merrion Street Upper you have a lovely view of the Georgian buildings to your right leading down to Merrion Square opposite the National Gallery, the essence of what those Georgian planners were trying to achieve. It is worth taking a few minutes to enjoy the square and admire the doors on the surrounding houses, a taste of Dublin indeed, and if the sun is shining down on you, you are doing well. En route to the galleries you pass the handsome Government Buildings on your left. Originally built by the British Administration, the foundation stone

was laid by King Edward VII in 1904. The first stages of the building were completed by 1911 and it was finally completed in 1922 just in time to be utilised by the new Irish Free State Administration. It was extensively refurbished in 1989-90 and now accommodates the offices of the Taoiseach and other leading political figures.

Georgian House Museum

Just as you come to the rear of Leinster House cross over the street to Merrion Square South and carry on down the length of the square admiring the fine Georgian doors as you go. Number 29 is facing you on the corner just across the road at the end of the square. Ahead of you on Mount Street Upper you see the delightful Georgian St Stephen's Church, a well known Dublin landmark known as the "Pepper Pot Church".

The Georgian House Museum is open from 10.00 a.m. - 4.30 p.m. 6 days a week, closed Mondays and

National Gallery and Museum

closed for two weeks at Christmas and on Good Friday. Admission €6.00.

Going through the house gives you a good idea of how people lived in those days, both upstairs and downstairs and an informative video highlights the different aspects of the realities of life in the house for all the occupants.

Owned by the Electricity Supply Board and run in partnership with the National Museum of Ireland it is furnished throughout with authentic Georgian furniture, wall paper and pictures supplied by the National Museum. You get a real feel for the original life of the building and how it looked. Some of the pictures are particularly interesting for their views of Dublin in the early 19th Century. This is genuine Georgian Dublin and all that is missing are the people, but the helpful attendants will do what they can to fill the gap. There is also a small café on site if you are in need of a caffeine fix.

To head back to the 21st century you go back up to street level and return to Merrion Square.

Just past Government Buildings you see some small metal railings and the entrance into the Natural History Museum and its collection of preserved animals and artefacts reflecting the wildlife and natural history, past and present, of the country. Being an island at the end of Europe Ireland missed out on some species, particularly snakes, but one species we did have was the Giant Irish Elk whose skeleton dominates the lower hall. Other non-Irish species are represented as well and if you are interested in natural history this is the place to come, an interesting contrast to what is exhibited on the other side of Leinster House.

Carrying on past the impressive rear facade of Leinster House brings you to the main entrance to the National

Gallery and its extensive displays of Irish and international art, both new and old. (Until 2016, when renovations to the main entrance are complete, access to the Gallery is by the Clare Street entrance round the corner). In 1853, William Dargan, a leading figure in the foundation of the Irish Railway System and an art collector, held a major art exhibition on the lawns of Leinster House. Shortly after a committee was set up to promote the Gallery which opened in 1864.

This is a very valuable asset for the city and a great place to spend a few hours if you are interested in art and culture. It holds a collection of approximately 15,000 works of art dating from the early 13th century to the 20th century. It covers all the major Irish artists, particularly Jack B. Yeats and it also covers international artists such as Rembrandt, Goya, Picasso and many others. In pride of place it holds the internationally famous Caravaggio's, The Taking of Christ. There has been much renovating and extending since its foundation but helped by many generous bequests and purchases the National Gallery is now a place of beauty to wander through and enjoy. There is also a deservedly well

regarded gallery shop and a good café on site to enhance the experience.

So having had your fill of culture you can return the way you came by the main entrance or go out the side entrance onto Clare Street and turn left. This brings you along the side of Trinity College grounds and leaves you at the bottom of Grafton Street. An alternative is to cross the road at the

traffic lights just by the exit, turn right and two minutes will bring you to the back entrance to Trinity College. You can meander back through the grounds and this will bring you to the front entrance to the college at College Green. If you use this route and are interested in all things Joycean, when you are at the gate look across the road and down towards the corner you will see the unusually spelled shop sign "Sweny". This is the site of the famous pharmacy mentioned in *Ulysses*. Still with its original fittings it is run by volunteers who sell books, lemon soap, as mentioned in *Ulysses* and run Joyce readings. Oscar Wilde's home is also just across the street on the corner of Merrion Square, it is quite possible that the Wilde family and Oscar himself would have used this pharmacy, all part of old Dublin.

3 To Trinity College and the Book of Kells

(Walking from the top of Grafton Street, 10 minutes)

Open: Mon – Sat: 9.30 a.m. – 5.00 p.m.. Sun:(May – Sept) 9.30 a.m – 4.30 p.m. Sun: (Oct – April) 12.00 p.m – 4.30 p.m. Summer Bank Holidays Open 9.30 a.m – 5.00 p.m, Winter Bank Holidays Open: 12 p.m. – 4.30 p.m. Admission €10, seniors/students €8.00, reduced group charges.

Leaving St Stephen's Green behind you, go straight down Grafton Street, carry on across the junction with Suffolk Street and Nassau Street and you approach Trinity College which is to your right. This is a popular exhibition and you may have to queue at peak times.

The first thing you notice approaching the college is the small, handsome Georgian building hidden behind the railings to your right which is the Provost's House. Dating from 1759 and still occupied by the Provost, it is one of the few Georgian buildings in the city still fulfilling its original purpose.

Founded in 1592 by Queen Elizabeth I of England and covering 45 acres, Trinity College is one of the most impressive buildings in the city centre. Together with the curved facade of the Bank of Ireland on the opposite side of the street, originally the Irish Houses of Parliament before the Act of Union in 1800, this is the

Trinity College, College Green. James Malton. Courtesy National Gallery of Ireland

and you come to the entrance to the Book of Kells Exhibition. This gives you a background history of the book and its creation and leads into the darkened room where two of the four volumes of this exquisite example of Celtic Art and Faith are displayed. The exact history of the book is not known and it is not complete but it is believed to be some 1200 years old. Sent to Dublin for safety in 1653 at the time of the Cromwellian War in Ireland it ended up in Trinity College a few years later where it has been protected and preserved down the centuries, quite an

architectural heart of Dublin. You enter the surprisingly small entrance gate, ahead of you, you see the striking Campanile, or Bell Tower, an iconic landmark of the college. The costs of construction of this were met by Lord John Beresford, Archbishop of Armagh. It was designed by Sir Charles Lanyon, who also designed the main building at Queen's University Belfast, and it was completed in 1853. Rumour has it that if a student passed under the tower when the bells were ringing he would not pass his exams, but that's a difficult one to prove. Keep right across the courtyard with its surrounding distinguished buildings and all the ghosts of its past students. The distinctive columned building to your right is the examination hall, beloved of students at that certain time of year. Exactly opposite is the chapel and beside that the dining hall, all full of their student stories and history. Follow the signs and go through to the adjoining smaller Fellows' Square to your right, turn left

achievement. It is difficult to take in the full glory of the book and its intricate detail on a simple visual examination, but it is worth trying and if you look carefully you may see some of the little flourishes or doodles at the end of some of the lines of text. A link with the human beings who created this masterpiece, but bring your specs!

You exit through the historic and atmospheric Long Room which is part of the Old Library of the College. Containing some 200,000 old volumes the Long Room was built between 1712 and 1732 by Thomas Burgh, an ex-student of Trinity College who also

marvellous Chester Beatty Library at Dublin Castle and Marsh's library beside St Patrick's Cathedral. As you leave the Trinity shop and its temptations, you find across the square in the futuristic concrete building the Douglas Hyde Gallery. Go into the building up the

Courtesy (and below) Board of Trinity College, Dublin

designed Collins Barracks in Arbour Hill, now part of the National Museum of Ireland. As Trinity College is a copyright library and entitled to a copy of any book published in the British Isles, its collection continually grows and in 1860 the library roof was raised to allow further shelving to accommodate the increased numbers of books, giving it its distinctive timber barrelled appearance today. In 1967, the striking Berkeley Library was built adjoining the Old Library to accommodate the ever increasing library and the demands of the modern student and this was followed by the Lecky library, the Hamilton library, and the James Ussher library in 1978,1992 and 2002 respectively.

With its thousands of old leather bound volumes and air of ancient academia and its busts of famous philosophers and writers keeping an eye on everything, it does fulfil the image of an early University with its emphasis on books and learning, a good home for the unique artefact that is the Book of Kells. And if books are your "thing", do not forget the

ramp to the right of the stairs and the gallery is just to the right as you enter the building. Admission is free and here you will find Contemporary Art, both Irish and international, in the open concrete space to balance the ancient art you have just enjoyed with the Book of Kells.

You can now return to the main entrance to continue your exploration of Dublin.

October, Michaelmas term. Walking through Front Arch, you can feel the anticipation of a new year. Front Square is rowdy with representatives from clubs and societies all jostling to sign students up for memberships. As a Fresher, you feel overwhelmed with the choice and find yourself agreeing to join a trampolining club, a debating society and a hiking group in the space of ten minutes. The following years you are wiser and vow to just observe but still get swayed by promises of free wine and cheese.

It is not hyperbole to say that you can feel the weight of history on your shoulders as a student in Trinity. You are after all in the company of greats – Jonathan Swift, Oscar Wilde, Samuel Beckett, they were all students here once. You are only eating sausages and chips but you are eating them in the grand surroundings of the Dining Hall, sitting at heavy wooden tables and watched over by portraits of frowning men

in powdered wigs. At the end of term you decide your fate in the 18th Century Exam Hall where a

conspicuous gap in the rows of desks exists underneath the portrait of Queen Elizabeth I. Rumour has it that any student sitting beneath her will fail and eventually, sick of protests, invigilators began to leave a space there. The libraries, the Berkeley, the Ussher, the Lecky and the Hamilton (more great alumni), are modern but stocked with a copy of every book ever published in Britain or Ireland, you feel there is nothing you cannot learn (if you manage not to fall asleep to the relaxing sound of others studying). It can take an outsider sometimes to make you realise how special your environs are. Possibly apocryphal, the story goes of a student who found a tourist wandering confusedly around the library stacks wondering which shelf would hold the Book of Kells.

Studying in the centre of the city made you feel a part of something big, like you had the world at your fingertips, and the multiculturalism of the student population only added to this feeling. There is no sweeter memory for me than sitting outside the Pav, our popular student bar, on a warm day, throngs of students all lounging on the grass and drinking cider. Cruelly, the weeks before exams were always the sunniest and trying to drag yourself away from the relaxed crowd and into the library was never fun and often fruitless. After the Pav, we would disperse to the usual haunts – The Ginger Man, Doyles, Kehoes – and while the night away with laughter and pints. With the end of term arrived the apex of the year, the Trinity Ball, and the excitement would mount as tickets were bought, tents were erected and the rumours about the acts were swapped. Listening to music in a spot-lit Front Square, surrounded by boys in tuxedos and girls in ball gowns, is a truly special experience and one that will stay with me.

With world class academic credentials, it is easy to see why Trinity is so attractive to students. To me however, its appeal was something more indefinable – the feeling, perhaps, of all that had gone before you and all that was ahead, that was yours to discover.

ELLEN HICKEY **BA English and Philosophy 2002-2007.**

4

To Temple Bar from Trinity College

(From Trinity, 5 minutes, from top of Grafton Street, 15 minutes)

Go straight out of the main entrance to Trinity, cross over to the porticoed Bank of Ireland Building and turn left. About half a kilometre along you pass the tiered brooding hulk of what is at present the Central Bank Building. Turning right here will bring you into the Temple Bar District.

Having crossed the road and if you have a few minutes to spare it is worth looking into the Bank of Ireland building and its public counters to admire the magnificent ceiling and plasterwork. This building was the original Irish Houses of Parliament until the Acts of Union with England in 1800 transferred all powers to Westminster in London. If you ask the usher you will probably be able to see the smaller room with its lovely barrel vaulted ceiling that was the original Irish House of Lords. One unfortunate aspect of the transfer of power and wealth to London was the decline of the importance and influence of Dublin on events in Westminster.

Construction on the Irish Houses of Parliament building began in 1729 and continued at intervals throughout the 18th century. After the Act of Union the building was taken over by the Bank of Ireland who made final alterations to the building and added the pillars which today give it its distinctive appearance.

If you have young people with you and you all want to be entertained, just beside the Bank of Ireland is the

"The Dublin Volunteers on College Green, 1779, Francis Wheatley." N.G.I.

National Wax Museum located in what was the Armoury Building of the bank and where gold and valuables were once held. The great and the mighty of Ireland are commemorated here and you will learn some history too.

But moving back to the present world you head into Temple Bar and its teeming variety of small shops and cafés and bars. Named after the Temple family who had a house and gardens in the area in the 17th century this is an old part of Dublin and the small streets reflect the original

medieval layout of the area. In the 1980s the government had planned to build a transport hub here and bought up much of the surrounding property which was by then in a fairly run down condition. While waiting for building to commence the buildings were let out to small businesses and craftsmen and the area developed a distinctive Bohemian air. When plans for the development were cancelled the properties were handed over to Temple Bar Properties to develop the area as a cultural hub and tourist area. Many important cultural organizations are now based here as well as many small indigenous businesses and there is a thriving pub scene and night scene in the evenings which can be quite raucous. Very different from the Book of Kells, but all part of the Dublin mosaic.

Temple Bar is also home to three markets at the weekends, the Book Market on Saturdays and Sundays and the Food Market and Designer Market on Saturdays only. The Book Market, 10.30 a.m. – 4.30 p.m., is the first market you come to in Temple Bar Square as you come down from Dame Street. Here book dealers set up their stalls and you can browse their stocks of secondhand and bargain books and music, have a coffee, enjoy the crowds and maybe find yourself a bargain.

You carry on down Temple Bar at the bottom of the square, cross over Eustace Street and in a little over 100m you will find the Temple Bar Food Market to your left in Meeting House Square beside Sycamore Street. Open 10.30 a.m – 4.30 p.m. on Saturdays, here you find high quality locally produced Irish foodstuffs including

cheeses, pastries, oysters, organic vegetables and other food exotica. Markets are very much part of the old tradition of this area and it is good to see a vibrant example of one thriving in this location, and the food is very tasty too!

The Design Market is about 250m from the Food Market and you continue along in your original direction towards Christchurch Cathedral along Essex Street East. You cross over Parliament Street into Essex Gate and you will find the Designer Market in Cow Lane, just beside the well regarded independent Gutter Bookshop. There are several design businesses in this area and the market itself is open from 10 a.m. – 5.00 p.m. on Saturdays. Here you will find a variety of handmade crafts and jewellery including ceramics, leather and other gifts, a good

place to buy that souvenir perhaps. Quite a contrast to the cows that were traded here in medieval times and the fish in adjoining Fishamble Street.

Going back up to Dame Street from Cow Lane you will find yourself very close to Dublin Castle and City Hall which are to your left and just across the road and Christchurch Cathedral is a short distance down the road to your right.

5

From Temple Bar to Dublin Castle, City Hall and Chester Beatty Library

(5 minutes walk from Temple Bar, from top of Grafton Street 15 – 20 minutes walk.)

Dublin Castle. Open: Mon – Sat 10.00 a.m. – 4.45 p.m, Open: Sundays and Bank Holidays 12.00 p.m – 4.45 p.m. Closed: Good Friday, Dec 24th – 28th incl, 1st January. Admission €4.50, students/seniors €3.50.

City Hall. Open: Mon – Sat 10.00 a.m. – 5.15 p.m.Closed Sundays and Bank Holidays. Admission to Exhibition €4.00.

From Temple Bar go back up to the main street (Dame Street), cross to the other side of the street and turn right. In about 5 minutes you approach City Hall, and just beyond it the main entrance to Dublin Castle, or you can meander through Temple Bar in your own time and end up in Cow Lane close to Dublin Castle.

Named after a medieval church located beside Dublin Castle, St Mary del Dam, Dame Street is a broad bustling artery of the city full of life and traffic. It is an easy walk to the complex of buildings that is Dublin Castle and the adjoining City Hall. Since the first Norman invasion of Ireland in the 1170s, this had been the seat of British power and administration in Ireland until the handover to the Irish Free State in 1922. The somewhat confusing array

of buildings you now see reflects the growth of what was once a Norman castle into a major administrative and tourist hub, still in active use today.

Here are held many of the Public Inquiries into our regular public scandals while state banquets and inaugurations are held in St. Patrick's Hall in the State Apartments. There are several conference centres in the complex including one in the striking Bedford Tower opposite the entrance to the State Apartments. The rather unattractive modern office building by the pedestrian entrance on Palace Street is occupied by the Revenue Commissioners who also run an interesting small museum under the Record Tower outlining the history of the Revenue's attempts to extract money from the citizens. Never a popular organ of state, nevertheless there would be no state without them. There is also a Garda Museum in the Record Tower, but check with the ticket office in the State Apartments for their opening hours. The gardens at the rear of the complex are a lovely quiet place to sit down in and reflect

on the environment, and there is the unique Chester Beatty Library to explore, admission free, so you could easily spend half a day at the complex, if not longer. If you have only time to do one thing in Dublin, this would be a good choice.

There are three entrances to the castle but the two principally used by visitors are the first one you come to, Palace Street Gate beside the AIB Bank and opposite the famous Olympia Theatre, and the main one, Cork Hill Gate, just beside the City Hall. At this gate the 1916 uprising started when the insurgents tried to rush the castle and shot the policeman on duty, their attempt failed and they retreated to the City Hall. The third one at Ship Street, behind the complex, is used for vehicular access to the rear of the building. Accessing through the pedestrian gate at Palace Street brings you round to the gardens at the rear and the Chester Beatty Library if you do not want to enter the castle itself.

Palace Street, named when the castle ceased to be a fortress and was considered more as a palace for the Lord Lieutenant of Ireland than a castle, is the main pedestrian access to the castle. Having entered the complex you turn right into Lower Castle Yard and the most striking building to your left is the neo-Gothic and charming Chapel Royal. Designed by Francis Johnston who also designed and built the General Post Office on O'Connell Street, building started in 1807 and completed in 1814. It is built on the

filled in area of the moat that surrounded the castle at this spot which caused many problems during the building and led to long delays and cost overruns with its soft foundations but what was completed is a gem with its intricate ceiling and its mini-Cathedral feeling. No longer a consecrated church, it is open to the public daily and there is a great sense of atmosphere inside it. With the opening of the Chapel Royal, Christchurch Cathedral just down the road diminished in importance which hastened its decay until its major restoration later on in the 19th century.

At the west end of the Chapel is the imposing Record Tower, the only one of the original Norman towers still standing. Dating from 1226 it was originally used as a high security jail for state prisoners. In 1814 it was converted to house the public records of Ireland, hence its name, and battlements were added to match the style of the newly built Chapel Royal. The same architect, Francis Johnston, was responsible for both jobs.

Opposite the Record Tower stood the Powder Tower. No longer standing, the basement area of the

tower, The Undercroft, can only be accessed with the guided tours of the castle and here you can see interesting stoneworks and some of the original fortifications of the castle. There is also a fair sized pool of stagnant looking water, part of the now underground River Poddle and the moat that used to surround the castle. This pool, into which water is still seeping, and the surrounding brickwork with its blocked off bridge and small staired access up into the original castle is a direct link with the early days of the building and its then uncertain future. Time and history move on however and so must we.

The fine Georgian buildings on this side of the square, known as the Treasury Buildings, were completed in 1720. Built originally as a government office it is today the office of the Comptroller and Auditor General and is the oldest continuously occupied office building in Dublin.

Leaving Lower Castle Yard you go into Upper Castle Yard. To your right you see the Castle Hall Conference Centre and the handsome Bedford

Tower and its cupola built on the site of the original Norman entrance to the castle. Completed in 1761 it is named after the Lord Lieutenant of the time, Lord Bedford, and today forms part of the conference facilities of the castle. With its matching gates of Fortitude and Justice, Bedford Tower gives a distinctive air to the Georgian regularity of the square. In 1907 the Irish Crown Jewels were stolen from the tower and have never been recovered, but they must be under a bed somewhere.

You enter the State Apartments through the main entrance to your left. Beautifully maintained by the Office of Public Works and sumptuously carpeted and furnished with period furniture and pictures, going round the apartments gives you a flavour of the luxury and routine that must have accompanied ceremonial life in the castle.

The rooms are beautiful, the reconstructed State Bedrooms, the Portrait Gallery, the Drawing Room, the Throne Room with its throne built for King George IV in 1821. All in mint condition and a tribute to the work done in maintaining them by the Office of Public Works. The most handsome room is St Patrick's Hall. Originally the ballroom for the castle, it is now used for state banquets and the inauguration of our presidents. Here in 2012 Queen Elizabeth II of England was entertained at a state dinner, the first state visit from a British Monarch since the British withdrawal in 1922, a historic moment indeed given the history between the two countries.

The room is magnificently decorated, the outstanding feature being the three paintings on the ceiling painted by Vincenzo Waldri in the 1780s depicting St Patrick converting the Irish to Christianity, King George III seated between Britannia and Hibernia and King Henry II receiving the submission of the Irish Chieftains in 1172.

The castle was the seat of British political power in Ireland for approximately 700 years but ultimately the forces of Irish Nationalism prevailed and it was handed over to

the new Irish Government in 1922 after the War of Independence from Britain. Fortunately it survived the turbulence of the ensuing Irish Civil War and hopefully will continue to survive for another seven centuries.

Having enjoyed the castle you can access the garden and buildings to the rear by exiting through the café by the entrance hall, enjoying a beverage on the way if needed, or you can access the garden by leaving at the main entrance and turning right into Lower Castle Yard. If you have not yet visited the Chapel Royal this is your opportunity, at the bottom of Lower Castle Yard turn right and this brings you to the garden and the Chester Beatty Library.

The garden, Dubhlinn Garden, though hard to imagine, is on the site of the original "Black Pool" after which Dublin is named. Here there was a small inlet off the River Poddle in which boats could be moored. The River Poddle now flows underground past the Lower Castle Yard and down into the Liffey and you can see pictures of it on Google, it also provided water for the moat of the castle. The garden was restored in the 1990s as was the castellated coach house at the end of the garden. In one corner of the garden is a small and dignified memorial garden honouring and naming those members of An Garda Síochána, the Irish police force, who have died in the service of the State. The coach house was built in its unusual form in 1833 to hide the view of the houses in the streets beyond and provide a pleasing vista of the garden when viewed from the castle and today is part of the conference facilities offered by the castle.

Looking at the back of the castle you can clearly see the layout of the Georgian building with the three towers incorporated into its structure, the most striking being the Record Tower beside the Chapel Royal. At the base of the Record Tower you will find the Revenue Museum and its history of money collection. The small centre octagonal structure is built on the site of the Black Clock Tower which collapsed in 1689, you would wonder a bit about the building standards of the day. On the left-hand side of the castle can be seen the base of the Bermingham Tower named after a prominent family of the 1300s. Damaged by an explosion in 1764, it was reduced to its sloping base before being reinstated as part of the castle complex. There was a square tower adjoining it which was also reduced to provide a gunnery platform.

There is a lovely row of Georgian buildings on the extreme left by Ship Street Gate, now occupied by the Revenue Commissioners, which gives a very 18th century feel to this part of the complex. The gate itself was designed and built by Francis Johnston, who also built the Chapel Royal, this is the main vehicular access to the complex. The final part of your visit to the complex, if you have time and are interested in the written word, has to be the Chester Beatty Library.

The Chester Beatty Library

Open: Mar – Oct: Mon – Fri 10.a.m. -5 p.m. Nov – Feb: Tues – Fri 10 a.m - 5 p.m. (Closed Mondays) Admission Free

Saturdays: 11 a.m – 5 p.m. all year
Sundays: 1 p.m – 5 p.m. all year
Closed: 1st January, Good Friday, 24th – 26th Dec incl, Monday Bank Holidays.

Just beside the garden in a modern building that was opened in 2000 is the world famous Chester Beatty Library. Chester Beatty, 1875-1968, was an American who made his money in mining. An interesting short film in the library gives an outline of his life. Obviously a man of culture and with a discerning eye he began collecting from an early age and by the time of his death he had amassed a unique collection of manuscripts and books, the earliest dating from 2700 B.C., as well as other historic artefacts.

It is impossible to describe the quantity and quality of the material held and displayed here, but it should not be missed. Uniquely for an Irish museum there is no Irish material, Trinity is where you go for that or the National Library, but there is unique material from Asia, the Middle East, North Africa and Europe. There are early copies of the Gospels and in the

world famous Islamic collection up to 6000 items alone. Not all the material is on display but what is on view is beautifully presented and carefully preserved. You will probably not understand a single word you see, but that is not the point, what is honoured here is the written word, its history, its beauty and its commonality between all races and creeds.

Having grown disillusioned with the Labour Government in post-war Britain and encouraged by tax concessions offered by the Irish Government, Chester Beatty moved his collection to Ireland in 1950 where he died in 1968 and was given a well deserved state funeral by a grateful nation. The collection was originally housed in his home in Ballsbridge before moving to its present site in 2000 and it is now rightly regarded as a world class collection.

The library is also home to the well renowned Silk Road Café with its varied menu and the library shop, a few euro spent here all helps to finance this marvellous asset for the city.

Having exhausted the attractions of Dublin Castle you can exit through Castle Hill Gate at the Bedford Tower and return back to Dame St and City Hall.

The City Hall

Rotunda: Open: Mon – Sat 10 a.m – 5.15 p.m.
Admission free.

Story of the Capital Exhibition. Open: Mon – Sat 10 a.m. – 5.15 p.m. Closed: Sundays and Bank Holidays.

Last admission 3.45 p.m. Admission Fee €4.00. Concessions apply.

This is a magnificent Georgian building with a continental feel to it, almost Roman, certainly not typical Dublin. You do not have to pay to enter the front hall and admire the handsome cupola with its twelve supporting pillars and plasterwork by Charles Thorpe. There is an admission fee to see the "Story of the Capital" Exhibition in the crypt but it is well laid out and worth seeing as it gives an interesting perspective of the evolution of the commercial and social life of the city since the Middle Ages.

The City Hall was built between 1769 and 1779 by the Guild of Merchants on the site of a 12th century church, Sainte Marie del Dame after which Dame Street was named. Originally called the Royal Exchange it was designed by the architect Thomas Cooley who was an associate of Francis Johnston who designed the Chapel Royal in Dublin Castle, Thomas Cooley was also involved in the design of the Four Courts across the river but died before work commenced and the work was finished by his great rival James Gandon. The grandeur of the building reflects the importance of trade in the city at this time and it was a meeting place for merchants to conduct their business with their goods being stored in the crypt beneath the building. It was conveniently located for access to the nearby River Liffey and the Customs House which was located on the site of the present day Clarence Hotel on the quays. In those days, before the building of the major bridges across the River Liffey, boats could still moor in this area of Dublin.

Taken over by Dublin Corporation in 1852, it was used for the civil administration of the city until 1995 when it transferred to its new base on nearby Wood Quay and the City Hall underwent extensive renovations to preserve the magnificent building we see today.

In 1922 It was used as the temporary headquarters of the new Provisional Irish Government after the British Government had handed over power and in the same year Michael Collins lay in state here for three days after his death in the Irish Civil war. It was also held for a time by rebels in 1916. At Cork Hill Gate just outside the front entrance, the first actions in the uprising of April of that year took place when the insurgents rushed the gate and attempted to take over Dublin Castle. The attempt failed and the British forces held the castle throughout the uprising but here the first fatality took place, a Royal Irish Constabulary policeman shot at the gate. The insurgents withdrew to City Hall and the rest is history. But this is not a martial building and makes no pretence to be, it glorifies the beauty of good architecture and the importance of trade, and you can get a good cup of coffee in the café in the crypt too.

The handsome building opposite City Hall was originally Newcomen Bank and is now a rates office. Designed by the architect Thomas Ivory in 1781 for what was then a private family bank owned by the Newcomen family, the bank failed in 1825 and the then Viscount Newcomen shot himself in his office. An interesting connection with the architect Thomas Ivory was that one of his students was James Hoban who was probably involved in some of the design of Newcomen Bank, he emigrated to America and went on to design the White House. Time to move on.

6 To Christchurch Cathedral and Dublinia Exhibition
(From Dublin Castle, 5 minutes walk, from top of Grafton Street, 25 minutes walk)

Christchurch Opening Hours: Monday – Saturday: March – May 9.00 a.m. – 6.00 p.m., June – Sept 9.00 a.m – 7.00 p.m., Oct – Feb 9.00 a.m. – 5.00 p.m.
Sunday Opening Hours: March – May 12.30 p.m. – 2.30 p.m., 4.30 p.m – 6.00 p.m., June – Sept 12.30 p.m. – 2.30 p.m.,4.30 p.m. – 7.00 p.m.,Oct – Feb 12.30 p.m – 2.30 p.m.
Admission Fee: Adults €6.00, children under 16 €2.00, concessions apply.

Leaving the Castle you cross the road and turn left. You carry on down the road until you come to the Cathedral and its distinctive bridge on your right.

Built on the site of an earlier Viking Church and dating from the 11th century the building was extensively renovated in the 1870s and it is now somewhat difficult to tell the difference between the original material and the renovations but much remains and you are standing in what is one of the earliest original buildings of Dublin. Originally sited in the centre of early Dublin and then surrounded by

clusters of buildings, progress has stripped away its original surroundings so that it now sits uneasily in what is for it the unnatural environment of a modern city.

This is a real relict of "Old Dublin" and the cathedral played a central part in the history of early Dublin and the spiritual and political administration of the city. It and St Patrick's Cathedral are the main cathedrals for the Church of Ireland and both play an active role in the life of the city. Its choir dates back to the 15th century and performs throughout the world and gives great pleasure to Dubliners throughout the year but particularly at Christmas time with its Christmas performances.

Not as grand as some of the mighty medieval cathedrals of England and Europe it nevertheless has a genuine feel of history about it and the fact that it is a practising church gives it a direct link back to its earliest days many centuries ago, an unusual feature in this ever changing digital age.

Being close to the castle meant that it always played an important part in the early history of Dublin. In medieval times it was the Diocesan Cathedral of Dublin and Glendalough and controlled large estates outside Dublin. The early British royals

worshipped here, in 1171 Henry II attended Christmas service here while in 1395 the Irish Chieftains of the four main provinces of Ulster, Connaught, Leinster and Munster held vigil here and paid homage to King Richard II, a decisive moment in Irish history.

A young pretender to the English throne, an English boy aged about 10 called Lambert Simnel, was crowned here as King Edward VI in 1487 having being put forward by forces opposed to the reign of Henry VII seeking support in Ireland for the Yorkist cause in the bitter English Civil War known as the "War of the Roses". It was a serious challenge but Henry VII triumphed at the Battle of Stoke Field in Lancashire later that year and his opponents and the opposing "King" were defeated. Unusually for a Tudor he spared Simnel who was given a job in the King's kitchen, history does not get much better than this really. Henry also showed leniency to the Irish rebels who had joined the Yorkist cause being unwilling to cause further unrest in the country, a good example of how important Ireland had

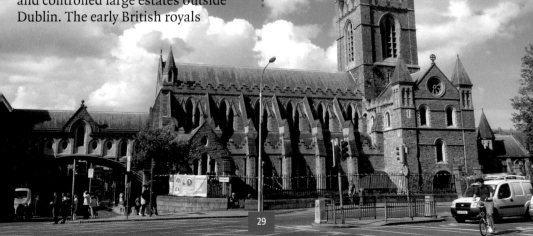

become in English politics.

In 1689 King James II attended mass here and for a brief period the cathedral returned to its old Catholic faith which had been disenfranchised by the Reformation of Henry VIII. Christchurch had survived the Reformation because of its importance in the fabric of the city. The old faith did not last long, after defeating James at the Battle of the Boyne in 1690, King William III gave thanks here and donated a magnificent collection of silver plate to celebrate his victory. That silver plate can now be seen in the crypt. He also reinstated the newly established Church of England and Ireland with the King at its head, the dream of a Catholic Ireland ruled by the Irish themselves faded until the 20th century. In this ancient space God and politics were never far apart.

The crypt is a major attraction of any visit to the cathedral. Dating from the late 11th or early 12th century it once hummed with the bustle of trading and commerce but having been extensively renovated in the 1990s it now houses many interesting monuments and artefacts relating to the cathedral. The Williamite plate is magnificent, there are the mummified remains of a cat and mouse mentioned by Joyce and in what must be one of the most unusual retail environments in Dublin you will find a café and the museum shop. Spend a few bob, it all helps to keep this magnificent old building going for another 1000 years. In complete contrast to the antiquity of the Cathedral is your next potential stop, Dublinia.

Dublinia

Cross over the street under the bridge, turn right, and you come to the entrance to the Exhibition just down the street to your left.

Open daily except Christmas, 23rd – 26th Dec and 17th March.
April – September: 10.00 a.m – last admissions 5.00 p.m..
October – March: 10.00 a.m. – last admissions 4.00 p.m.
Admission Fee: Adults €8.50, Child €5.50, Student/Senior €7.50, Family (4) €24.00

This is a great place for kids. Unlike Christchurch Cathedral or Dublin Castle which were definitely not laid out to entertain young people, this place was. With its well laid out sections and interactive audio and visual displays and living tableaus of daily life in Viking and Medieval Dublin, not that attractive by the look of things, it entertains and educates the visitor at the same time. Laid out in three sections that cover Viking Dublin, Medieval Dublin and the history and science of the archaeology itself you can follow the floor plan and enjoy the exhibits which give a real flavour of the

period concerned. It brings history to life in a way that the other attractions around Dublin cannot do and children and adults will come away with a better idea of what life really was like in Dublin in those days.

The exhibition building itself was originally the Synod Hall for Christchurch Cathedral, a place where the clergy met to discuss the affairs of the cathedral. The Synod Hall and connecting bridge were built at the time of the major restoration in the 1870s. Built on the site of the medieval church of St Michael's and All Angels the church itself has been demolished but the sturdy and large church tower remains and if you have the energy it is worth the climb to the top which is enclosed and protected from the elements. From here there is a great view of the surrounding city.

7 St Patrick's Cathedral and Marsh's Library
(5 minutes walk from Christchurch)

Opening hours: March – October: Monday – Friday 9.30 a.m – 5.00 p.m, Saturday 9.30 a.m – 6.00 p.m, November – February 9.30 a.m – 5.00 p.m
Sunday – 9.00 a.m – 10.30 a.m, 12.30 p.m – 2.30 p.m, 4.30 p.m – 6.00 p.m.
Sunday (November – February) 9.00 a.m – 10.30 a.m., 12.30 p.m. – 2.30 p.m.
Admission Fee: Adults €6.00, Seniors/Students €5,00, Family (4) €15.00, group discounts apply (min 10)

On exiting Christchurch or Dublinia cross the road at the traffic lights and proceed down Nicholas Street opposite, in a few minutes you come to St Patrick's Square and the cathedral.

Just a few minutes walk from Christchurch you come to its sister cathedral, St Patrick's. It is most unusual to have two cathedrals in such close proximity to each other in what was then a small medieval city. To build such a building in the present day would stretch the resources of any organization, the fact that our medieval forefathers could raise the resources to build it is impressive. Why the archbishop of the day, John Comyn, made the decision to build the second cathedral outside the city walls is not entirely clear but it probably had a lot to do with clerical and lay politics, the existing set up in Christchurch which was run by the Augustinians and the recent Norman invasion and the new king on the block, Henry II.

Built in the early 13th century, it is over 100 years younger than Christchurch and there was rivalry from the beginning. It was not until 1300 when they signed the "Composicio Pacis", which recognized both institutions as diocesan cathedrals, that peace reigned between them and today St Patrick's is the national cathedral for the Church of Ireland and Christchurch is the seat of the archbishop and the diocesan cathedral for Dublin and Glendalough.

Built on the location of a well associated with St Patrick believed to have been located somewhere in St Patrick's Park, the site was venerated

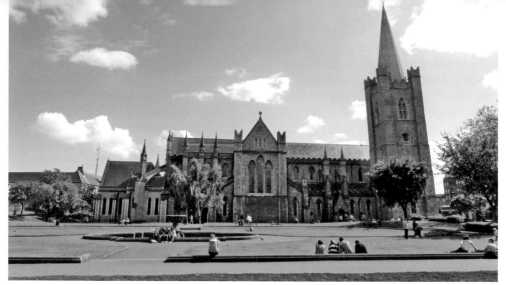

Opposite page, image courtesy St. Patrick's Cathedral, Dublin

long before the city of Dublin existed. It is not possible to be sure if St Patrick ever visited the site in the 5th century, but oral tradition can be accurate and tradition also suggests that St Patrick landed in the Arklow area to make contact with the local tribes while travelling North at that time, whatever happened he certainly made a big impression on this area.

Christchurch is set in what is now a busy urban environment but St Patrick's has a much more peaceful air about it. Set off the main road in St Patrick's Close and with the charming St Patrick's Square to one side, on a sunny day this is a good place to be, the cathedral completely at one with its surroundings. The lines of the building are cleaner than Christchurch and it looks in good condition though as with Christchurch it has been extensively restored. She has the look of being the "younger sister" to Christchurch and she is trying to make an impression, and she does.

As with Christchurch much of what you see is the result of major renovations undertaken in the 1860s by one of the ubiquitous Guinness family, Sir Benjamin Lee Guinness, the father of Lord Ardilaun who helped to open St Stephen's Green to the public. The building was on the verge of collapse and a valuable service to the city was rendered by preserving this marvellous old building for the future. As with Christchurch it is difficult to discern the original from the renovated but the spiritual essence of the church is preserved and maintains the Christian tradition of the church which stretches back from its earliest days to the present day.

This is the largest church in the island of Ireland and coming in from the main entrance and looking down the cathedral is an impressive sight. There is a lot to see in the cathedral, as with Christchurch you get a strong feeling of the Irish involvement in centuries of "partnership" with Britain and her Empire. Throughout the walls there are plaques and monuments commemorating the Irish regiments and individuals of the British Army and the long forgotten colonial wars they were involved in. From the walls of the North Transept hang the dusty and fading flags of those regiments. More recent wars are not forgotten, there is a Roll of Honour for the dead of the First World War and every November there is a remembrance service for all Irishmen who have fallen in war. It is not all dead history, the British Army still has two Irish Regiments, the Irish Guards and the Royal Irish Regiment, many recruits come from England and Northern Ireland, but recruits still come from the South and the history carries on.

In the cathedral as well as the military memorabilia are fine burial monuments and statues to local worthy citizens, the common man and woman not so well remembered perhaps but this is a common situation with most famous cathedrals and churches. The Order of St Patrick's, a dormant British order of chivalry associated with the British administration of Ireland together with its regalia and helmets is remembered in the choir but one of the most recognized memorials is the one to John Swift, dean of Christchurch from 1713-45. Famous for his acerbic writings and satire as well as *Gulliver's Travels*, on his death in 1745 he bequeathed the bulk of his monies to the setting up of a hospital nearby for the mentally insane. The hospital exists to this day in James's Street not far from the Guinness Storehouse and is an important part of the fabric of the city. He is commemorated with a fine bust and memorial and rests with his companion Stella underfoot just near the entrance door.

The cathedral is a good space to be in, the stained glass windows of the Lady's Chapel and the fine stained glass windows throughout the cathedral give a pleasing sense of colour and light to what would otherwise be a somewhat stern Gothic interior. Dating from the 1200s and influenced by the design of Salisbury Cathedral in England which was being built around the same time, it has been extensively restored since its original construction. Being built on a damp site between what was then two branches of the river Poddle, outward leaning walls and a collapsing tower not to mention a serious fire in 1362 means that the building has had many problems in its life, but it must be said that for this stage of her existence the old lady is looking pretty good.

In its earliest days it was also an educational establishment and the first University of Ireland was founded here in 1311, it survived until the Reformation in 1530 when it ceased to exist. These were turbulent times but by 1592 a protestant Trinity College had been founded by Queen Elizabeth I and the history of third level education marched on in Ireland without St Patrick's. But the adjoining St Patrick's Grammar School was set up in 1432 to educate the choristers of the cathedral,

a roll it still fulfils today, and is a thriving school, the ancient link continues.

The cathedral is famous for its music provided by its cathedral choir and the St Patrick's girl choristers and they provide music for services in the cathedral as well as touring and giving concerts. The tradition of liturgical music in the great cathedrals of Europe is a valuable one and maintained to the highest standards by the choirs of St Patrick's and Christchurch. The choristers of both cathedrals provided the choir for Handel's first performance of the Messiah in Fishamble Street in 1742 and no doubt he would be happy to use the present choirs if that situation rose again.

Comparing the two, Christchurch seems more ancient, its location less suitable though in its day it was in a prime location. Near Dublin Castle and the centre of political power and activity sitting comfortably within the city walls, then St Patrick's was the outsider, sitting beyond the city walls and trying to steal Christchurch's glory. But now St Patrick's rests more comfortably in its environment, younger, better looking. Both have their respective charms and both in their different ways reflect the ethos of their Church of Ireland Creed and its long association with what was for many centuries of their existence the British administration of the Irish nation. Trying to understand Irish history is no easy matter but these two cathedrals, encompassing the history of the religion of the country, both pre

and post Reformation, and the medieval and later history of the country, are a standing testimony to that history and culture and enjoying and appreciating them will give you some understanding of the complexities involved.

Marsh's Library

Open every day (except Tuesday and Sunday): 9.30 a.m. – 5.00 p.m., Saturday: 10.00 a.m. – 5.00 p.m., Closed Bank Holidays.
Admission Fee: €3.00, seniors/students €2.00,

Exiting the cathedral's entrance and just to your left is Marsh's Library, a fascinating example of authentic early Georgian Dublin. Commissioned by the Archbishop of Dublin, Narcissus Marsh, it was opened in 1707. This was the Google type operation of its day, a state of the art library with an extensive range of books covering many different topics, a depository of information in one location, available to all and the first public library in Ireland – if you were literate of course.

The library is a valuable research tool containing books dating from the 16th to the 18th century and includes Archbishop Marsh's own library and material that was accumulated by purchase and donation. Today you can see the ancient leather-bound volumes on their original hand-built shelves in their original environment. You have moved from the 21st century back to the 18th century but at least you do not have to read the books and you can just enjoy the items that have been put out on display.

Based on the Bodleian library in Oxford, it was designed by Sir William Robinson who was also involved in the design of several important buildings in Ireland including work on the Upper Yard in Dublin Castle and the Royal Hospital in Kilmainham. It was built in two stages with the first gallery and the old reading room probably being built between 1703-05 and the second gallery added sometime around 1708-09. The first stage contained an apartment on the lower floor for the Keeper when built, still the case today and the remainder of the lower level is now used as a lecture room for the library which came into formal existence with the passing of an Act of Parliament in 1707.

Narcissus Marsh was an erudite Englishman who was Archbishop of Dublin between 1694-1703 during which time the library was commissioned. His unusual Christian name must have caused him problems in school as a boy but his brothers must have had a worst time. Named by their parents after people mentioned in Saint Paul's epistles his brothers were named respectively Epaphroditus and Onesiphorus, what their school friends made of this history does not relate.

He was interested in the Irish language, despite opposition from the government who associated it with nationalist sentiment, and promoted its study in college to enable his clergy to converse with the natives in their own language and facilitate conversion to the Church of Ireland. He also arranged for the first Irish translation of the Old Testament in 1685.

He was appointed Provost of Trinity in 1673 and in his time there found that the running of the library, and the arrangements for people to borrow books from the library, were not satisfactory. This encouraged him in his idea of setting up a public library run independently from the clerical authorities. He does not seem to have been a very popular man and his idea ran into opposition from the church authorities, including Jonathan Swift, who were not happy with the removal of property and control from their power, but he achieved his aim and the library opened in 1707, open to the public and controlled by an Act of Parliament. Today it runs as a charitable trust and stands as a permanent memorial to the Archbishop whose name and library is as much associated with St Patrick's Cathedral as Jonathan Swift's is. No doubt Mr Swift would have something to say about that if he was around today.

It is a fascinating place to experience if you are interested in books and an authentic taste of Georgian Dublin. Together with the library at Trinity and the Chester Beatty library it typifies the literary culture of the city and its interest and respect for the written word. The spoken word has always been celebrated and enjoyed in this city, in these libraries the written word is preserved and cherished.

You now have a choice of returning to Christchurch and carrying on with the guide from there, taking a hop-on bus from the entrance to the cathedral to wherever you wish to go, or if you wish to return to Grafton Street it is a 15 minute walk from here.

To return to Grafton Street: Turn left as you leave the library or the Cathedral and leave St Patrick's Close to join Kevin Street Upper passing the backyard to Kevin Street Garda Station (the former site of the Archbishop's palace for the cathedral). Cross Bride Street to join Kevin Street Lower. Cross Wexford Street to join Cuffe Street and this brings you to the corner of Stephen's Green, turn left to bring you to the top of Grafton Street.

If you have returned to Christchurch you have just left the entrance to the cathedral and the tour carries on as follows:

The Guinness Storehouse

(From Dublinia/Christchurch, 15 minute walk, from top of Grafton St, 40 minute walk)
Rejoin the main road and cross it, keep to the left-

hand road at the traffic lights (Cornmarket) and this brings you onto Thomas Street. The Storehouse is about a 15 minute walk along here on the left hand side down Crane Street. The directions are well signposted.

You may prefer to take the hop-on bus at this stage or the 123 bus, make sure you have lots of change as exact fares must be paid and they do not give out change, but the walk is an interesting one and recommended.

If you are walking and if you have twenty minutes to spare, an interesting diversion is to call into the medieval church of St Audoen which you will see shortly after leaving Christchurch on your right. If you want to visit it just turn right having left Christchurch and stay on this side of the road. Just below the church and accessed by passing the front door of the church and going down steps to the street below is the only major section of the city walls still standing. Going down

to have a look at it will give you a good idea of the scale and appearance of the original city walls.

St Audoen's Church and City Walls
(From Christchurch 5 minutes walk)

Open: 25th April – 23rd October, Daily 9.30 a.m. – 5.30 p.m., Last admission 4.45 p.m.
Admission Free.
At weekends the garden in front of the church may be closed preventing access to the city walls.If that is the case then on exiting Dublinia turn left,turn right down St Michael's Close, when you come to the main road at the bottom (Cook Street) turn left and you will see the city walls about 100 metres down to your left.

Dedicated to the 7th century Bishop of Rouen in Normandy, France, the present church, built between 1181 and 1212, which seems to have been a long time in building, is believed to be built on the site of an earlier church. The connection with France being the then Norman Archbishop of Dublin, John Comyn who was

chaplain to Henry II, King of England, who had only recently invaded Ireland (1172) and who also controlled extensive lands in France, among his many titles being that of the Duke of Normandy. John Comyn replaced St Laurence O'Toole as Archbishop of Dublin and must have taken an active interest in the building of the church. He was also responsible for building St Patrick's Cathedral and undertaking renovations in Christchurch Cathedral where he is buried.

Run by the Office of Public Works this is still a working Church of Ireland church. The church has been much altered over the centuries but it has now been restored and is well maintained by the OPW who have an exhibition on the church in the reroofed Eastern section of the church previously known as St Anne's Chapel. The authentic sense of history within the chapel is augmented by the gravestones and monuments within it. Old churches and cathedrals always seem to live so well with their history, far more so than more recent buildings, they can connect you to the past and the people and the spirituality of that time. This place certainly does that.

As previously related, to see the city walls, go to the front of the church, enjoy the little garden there, pass the front door and follow the stepped lane beside the church bringing you down to the lower street level and the wall. You go out through St Audoen's Gate, built in the 13th century. Looking back at the restored section of the wall gives you a good idea of the height and scale of the original. Standing in the gateway is one of the few places in Dublin that gives you a genuine link to the original medieval city, it can hardly have changed at all since those days.

The walls played an important role in the early life of the city as the city was then under constant threat from the indigenous population in the outlying areas beyond the fortified area around Dublin known as the Pale. As you head towards the Guinness Storehouse you see another small section of freestanding wall on Cornmarket.

Towards Guinness Storehouse

Returning to Cornmarket and carrying on towards the Guinness Storehouse down Thomas Street you get a good taste of modern street life in Dublin away from the tourist hotspots. There are many different types of retail outlets with different ethnic outlooks. If you have time divert down Meath Street and enjoy the variety of retail life and Dublin life there. This is the heart of old Dublin and the area known as the "Liberties" where the original Dublin accent and Dublin character still prevails together with the street trader and their stalls and great bargains. Opposite Meath Street is the National College of Art and Design training generations of talented young artists. There is free admission to their Gallery which can be accessed by going through the archway off Thomas Street and turning left. The diversity of modern Dublin is apparent. A further short distance on you pass the sombre facade of St Catherine's Church. Now a deconsecrated Church of Ireland church it was built between 1760 and 1769 on the site of an earlier church and is now an evangelical and community centre run within the Church of Ireland. In front of it Robert Emmet, a famous Irish patriot, was executed in 1803 after his failed uprising against the Crown Forces.

As you approach Crane Street and the Guinness Storehouse you see a tall lighthouse-shaped building to your right. This was originally a windmill built for Roe's distillery, now extinct, in 1757. Minus its sails it stands as a distinctive landmark for the area.

And so you come to Crane Street and follow the signs to bring you to the Guinness Storehouse. Set amidst the cobbled streets and towering warehouses of the Guinness complex, this is one of the major visitor attractions of Dublin and Ireland. This ubiquitous Irish brand seems to be as much part of our Irish culture as our Round Towers, yet it is owned by an international conglomerate! But Dublin is part of Guinness and Guinness is part of Dublin.

The Guinness Store House

Open Daily: 9.30 a.m. – Last admissions 5.00 p.m.,
Closed: Good Friday and 24th, 25th, 26th December.
July and August: Last admissions 7 p.m.
Admission Fee: Adults €18.00, Seniors €14.50,
Student over 18 €14.50, Student under 18
€12.00, Children 6 – 12 €6.50, Family €42.50

Laid out over seven levels in what was an enormous fermentation plant you travel through the whole story of the history and production and distribution of this famous stout. Here you will find the definitive Guinness souvenir shop, cafés, and at the top of the building, the Gravity Bar with its "view to die for". It is difficult to understand how one brand of stout can come to represent a country but Guinness has managed to do it. Part of its success has always been that it has a good reputation for caring for its workers and for the surrounding community. In the 19th and early 20th centuries, in those more difficult days, a job with Guinness was a job for life with good working conditions and health care. Sir Arthur Guinness

played a major role in opening St Stephen's Green to the public in 1880 and in 1890 Edward Cecil Guinness, the first Lord Iveagh, set up the Iveagh Trust which provided much needed social housing and other facilities for the local community. The company always had a good reputation with a contented workforce producing a good product, a good formula and it worked. It has also had clever and individual advertising. The Toucan advertising from the 1930s, some of which can be seen in the Storehouse, is still effective today and the tradition is maintained with its striking television and film advertisements. There are few Irishmen who have not enjoyed their pint of Guinness at one time or another.

The highlight of your tour has to be the drink and the view from the Gravity Bar. This is about the best view of Dublin you are going to get and is almost worth the admission price itself. All around you Dublin stretches out to the Dublin Mountains and in the far distance the Sugar Loaf and the Wicklow Hills. If you look carefully you can see many of the places you have visited, this is a fitting place to end your guide with Dublin at your feet with all its charm and character, and the odd blemish. Hopefully you have enjoyed seeing the town and the attractions around Grafton Street and this guide will travel home with you and be a souvenir and memory of your trip here, and who knows, maybe in a few years time it might encourage you to return and see it all again and you might end up in the Gravity Bar with that famous drink in your hand, just like the British Queen, Sláinte!